Hands Washing Water

Also by Chris Abani

Chris Abani

Hands Washing Water

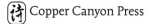 Copper Canyon Press

Cover art: Leonard Freed, "Fire Hydrant," Harlem, 1963. Silver print,
10⅜" × 6¾" inches. Courtesy of the artist and Lee Gallery.

Copper Canyon Press is in residence at Fort Worden State Park in
Port Townsend, Washington, under the auspices of Centrum
Foundation. Centrum is a gathering place for artists and
creative thinkers from around the world, students of all
ages and backgrounds, and audiences seeking
extraordinary cultural enrichment.

LIBRARY OF CONGRESS CATALOGING-IN-PUBLICATION DATA

Abani, Christopher.
Hands washing water / Chris Abani.
p.   cm.
ISBN 1-55659-247-7 (pbk.: alk. paper)
I. Title.
PR9387.9.A23H36   2006
821'.914 — DC22
2006013303

3 5 7 9 8 6 4 2
FIRST PRINTING

COPPER CANYON PRESS
Post Office Box 271
Port Townsend, Washington 98368

www.coppercanyonpress.org

For

Horace Tapscott, Richard Fulton, Wole Soyinka

and my friend

Ron Gottesman

whose hearts have changed the world

ACKNOWLEDGMENTS

Some of these poems appeared in:
Beyond the Valley of the Contemporary Poets, The Big Bend Sentinel,
Calabash (U.K.), *Crate, Eclipse, Fugacity 05* (N.Z.), *Hayden's Ferry Review,*
Main Street Journal (U.K.), *Oban 06* (N.Z.), *On Broken Wings*
(ed. Unoma Azuah) (U.K.), *Ploughshares, The University News* (N.Z.),
and the PEN American Center Web site.

I would like to thank David St. John, who has been such a gift;
Percival Everett, Ron Gottesman, Carol Muske-Dukes, Maurya Simon,
Kwame Dawes, Juan Felipe Herrera, Terrance Hayes, Natasha Tretheway,
Tayari Jones, Adonis, Zaia Alexander, Andrew Rubin, Kate Gale and
Mark Cull, and everyone at Copper Canyon Press,
particularly Michael Wiegers.

Also, much thanks to the generous folks at Lannan Foundation.

Contents

Hands Washing Water

One

*I have never found a way to separate art from
the act of living.*

John Outterbridge

Auckland

the only Land... I can claim for sure...
(is) lodged between my toes
Hone Tuwhare

This is the measure of it.

Norfolk pines on Stanley Point,
like pagodas on an imagined horizon,
descend the hill slowly, dip
travel-weary feet in the saltwater.

On North Head, where the rock curves away
like the broadside of a giant back, is a cave
that catches the sweetness of the full moon
rising over the lips of the waves.
An ancient buried there stands in my mind
blowing a conch; calling, calling, calling

the way Tutanekai played that horn
with a desire and tenderness Miles never could.
Each note a drop, like pounamu on a string,
pulling Hinemoa across the water.

In front of St. Andrew's is a rock, recalcitrant
in the way only old stone can be. Until Yang
Lian's tears watered it with all the purity of rain.
That rock is a tongue chanting the names of the dead
to all who pass, and even those who don't.

My kiwi friends and I make fun of tourists. Coming
up with new schemes to fleece them. We plan to get
a matching pair of fluffy Kerry Blue terriers and
pretend they are sheepdogs – a new species crossing
sheep and dogs into two prototypes: Baawoof and Grendel.

The museum on the sacred hill reassures
me that all old cultures are more the same.
Here there are the two staples of my people, Igbo:
yams and kumara, the limbs and intestines of
a sacrificed ancestor who gave us life.

I enter the room with the artifacts,
tracing the lines cut on
a Maori ancestor's face. I remember
in this my grandfather's face, cut deep
like the grooves scoured by blood,
marking him as a warrior, and I
am closer to home than I have been
for a very long time.

Tapa cloth against my skin recalls
a blue night in Timbuktu, where a lone
star filled the maw of darkness.

In a radio station studio, Yang Lian and I
face off like warriors. But this meeting
is an embrace, not death. And his words:
Before I came to Auckland, the sea was a distant

Idea. When I came to Auckland, I put my hand
In the sea and felt only the points of separation.
It took five years for me to find the sea inside my body —
This is true: words are bridges linking people
defeating the abrupt betrayal of piers.

Tin of cocoa
Tin of cocoa
Tin of cocoa
Car tow-er
signal me that another ancient language is
being mangled in the clumsy mouths
of a newer people. Yet even this
gesture is better than the erasure
my language suffers, because all
gestures point to a horizon of possibility.

Kauri trees are chained to the earth on Queen Street
where the land ends in the sea. I wonder if these
chains keep the kauri from returning to their relatives —
sperm whales calling in dreams the path to freedom.

All of me meets here, an alchemy of parts —
the Pacific of residence, the Atlantic of birth,
the English of heritage, and a culture, like mine,
old enough to have words for birthing the earth.

The glass arch of Grafton Bridge curves around
me in light, like the dazzle of the sun through

a dragonfly's wings, protecting me from
the old cemetery below. And that brilliance,
I think, will light my way home.

Antwerp

I

The way a body gives in to a sigh, gentle
as a tongue of surf on a morning beach,
this thing in the cobbled streets pushes up
against me. I give in to the cry:
this is your African blood
grouting these stones. Tunnels, freshly dug,
dip away in apology, remorse crumbling into earth.

II

In the distance, Rubens points away to the sadness:
a cathedral leaning on one tower like a cripple,
a mendicant before heaven's grace beating its chest.
A woman in tropical fabric bright against her
skin comes toward me, smiling as she points
away to Rubens pointing away — in the distance.

III

And churches, more churches, so many: yet
everyone, everything pretends the sacred
is dead here. But at every turn a Virgin in a niche
high on a wall smiles down ironically at me:
Don't believe it, she says, don't.

IV

Standing in the magnificent roofless cathedral
of the red-light district, I watch the faithful
walk the Stations of the Cross, bent from the heavy
hard of wood. Dark Madonnas staring
from each window tell me, She is right.

Durban, South Africa –
Some Notations of Value

Metal giraffes march up the bluff
toward the lighthouse. In the moonlight,
whales, or their ghosts, litter the sand.

There is a museum by the park that houses
apartheid; contained in stiff wax dummies.

The tour bus stops on the road's edge.
On the right a black town, the left Indian.
Pointing he says: This is the racial divide.

Stopping at the bar, the drink menu offers –
Red's Divas only five rand each.

Each night the pounding sea reminds me
that, here, women are older than God.

These people carry their dead with them,
plastering them onto every met face.

Yet love hums like tuning forks
and the fading spreading sound
is the growth of something more.

Their absence is loud and I long
for the confetti flutter of butterflies.

Abattoirs litter the landscape with the sinister
air of murder, signs proclaiming: *Zumba Butchery,*
as though this is where the Zumba's blood-
lust got the better of them.

The air conditioner in my room hums
a dirge to a sea too busy spreading rumors.

Death skips between street children
playing hopscotch in the traffic.

The woman singing in Zulu, in a Jamaican bar,
is calling down fire, calling down fire.
There is no contradiction.

Hanging in Egypt with Breyten Breytenbach

There are stones even here
worn into a malevolence by time
gritting the teeth and tearing
the eye with the memory.

Out in the desert, the wind
is a sculptor working the ephemera
of sand. Desperately editing steles
to write the names of thousands of slaves
who died to make Pharaoh great.
It is a fool's game.

And we are like the blind musician
at the hotel who tells us with a smile:
I'll see you later.

The guard at the pyramid eyes me.
Are you Egyptian? he demands,
then searches my bag for a bomb.
At the hotel they speak Arabic to me,
don't treat me like the white guests,
and I guess, even here, with all
the hindsight of history we haven't
learned to love ourselves.

I cannot crawl into the tombs, and cannot
explain why. How do you say: In my country
they buried me alive for six months?
And so you lie and tell yourself this is love.
I am protecting the world from my rage.

Rabab tells me: We know how to build graves
here. I nod. I know. It is the same all over Africa.

Do you have a knife? Do you have one?
the guards at the museum ask Breyten and me,
searching us. We call this on ourselves. We
are clearly political criminals.

I trace the glyphs chipped into stone.
As a writer I am drawn to this. If I could
I too would carve myself into eternity.
Breyten watching me says: Don't tell me
you've found a spelling mistake in it!

A line of miniature statues is placed
into the tomb to serve the pharaoh.
One for each day of the year. Four hundred.
The overseers are a plus. I think
even death will not ease
the lot of the poor here.

Statues: it seems the more I search the world
for difference the more I find it all the same.

Perhaps the Buddha was a jaded traveler too
when he said we are all one.

Mona argues about who should pay
to see the mummies. It isn't often I can
treat a girl to a dead body, Breyten insists.

A woman nearby tells her husband she can see
dead bodies at work. Why pay?
Do you think she works in a hospital? I ask.
That or the U.S. State Department, Breyten agrees.

From the top of Bab Zwelia, flat rooftops
spread out like a conference of coffee tables.
Broken walls, furniture, pots, litter the roofs
like family secrets sunning themselves.
Two white goats on a roof chew
their way through the debris.

On the Nile, Rabab sings in Arabic, tells me
she wants to be Celine Dion.
She is my sister calling me home to Egypt.
Perhaps one day I will be ready.
For now it is enough to know I can
be at home here.

Poem

a.m.
Summer. Corner of Sixth Ave and Twenty-second.
It's like walking through a dirty wet sponge.
If there was ever a case for public showers —

In cement turning green with envy, Michelangelo's
David stands barely tall enough to play for the NBA.
A disapproving terrier goes on his leg, sniffs; trots off.

p.m.
Clouds occlude an already dirty sky.
Rain? The guy in Starbucks says: Oh my God!
I'm still here. Didn't make the rapture.
From ceiling-vaulted loudspeakers, Pavarotti intervenes
in the only voice God will listen to.
But what does it mean?
             To always lose things you cannot name?
Truth, an old friend said. Truth is
             the pressure of rain on a linen shirt.

Today the mail didn't come —
             Damn! I need that check
or there'll be no lights over the door.
And a hummingbird, circling the bulb on the porch.
No! Wait a minute. That's L.A.
             Not here. Not this poem.

later p.m.
But still there is something
            about ships and strangers in the night. No!
Again, wait.
            That is some other Frank. This one knew
about the fathomless depths of a tide.

This desire is like the smug weight of a new glass
marble, green flecked with purple,
            in a schoolboy's lint-heavy pocket.

The homeless man on the corner,
hair wound around his head: a turban;
            beard heavy as Tagore's, yells Hafiz at passersby:

*This sky / where we live / is no place / to lose your wings /
            so love. Love. Love.*

I throw a quarter in his cup.
            You know! he exclaims. I do, I reply.
New York is everywhere...
Perhaps I'll find my way. Still.

Letter to the Editor

Dear Sir/Madam,

The main thrust of my missive is to complain about the town of Marfa and how it has treated me. In this, Sir or Madam, I refer mainly to the hoax of the Marfa Lights. When I came to this town, it was with the understanding that there was a paranormal phenomenon referred to on the side of the building next to the Pueblo Market as a supernatural event, and possibly even an extraterrestrial experience. I have been in your rather lovely town now for three weeks and despite numerous visits to the viewing station, and several late night trips down dark and deserted farm roads, I have encountered only suicidal hares and bored border patrol officers, whom I now understand were looking for aliens of a different dimension, but alas, no Marfa lights.

Many people in town have assured me that they have seen these lights (and I am not here referring to the fading red taillights on Highway 67), or that they have indeed interacted with these orbs of mystery. These accounts, rather than reassure me, make me wonder if there is something in the air or water here as not only do people see these lights but, also according to your paper, they now see the Guadalupe Virgin in a fold of rock on Chinati Peak.

I know my tone may seem somewhat whiny and even curmudgeonly, but I am writing this with the best intentions as I feel that this misrepresentation may cause your town much embarrassment. My suggestion in this case has a twofold benefit. One is that it would satisfy discerning tourists seeking value for money, and the second is that it would provide character-building work for Marfa youths as well as serve to keep them out of trouble. And this is my suggestion: that the town hire teenagers, arm them with flashlights, and have them cycle up and down the farm roads abutting the Chinati Mountains. This way we can all have an authentic experience.

Speaking of the Chinati Mountains, I would like also to complain about the Chinati Foundation. While this foundation and Mr. Judd were well intentioned, I do not see why their tour guide would prevent me and my family from having our lunch on the metal picnic tables provided by the thoughtful Mr. Judd. This situation left me most puzzled, particularly since with over a hundred of such tables, there were enough for everyone.

In addition, some of the exhibits are not kept well. I refer to a certain Russian exhibit. The paint in the building it is housed in is peeling and there are shreds of newspapers dating back to the nineteen forties strewn everywhere. If they need a new janitor, I am happy to provide a few names of kind folk I have encountered in my stay here. I also hate to point out the possibility that this exhibit points to the fact that the Chinati Foundation is a hotbed for Communism. Now more than ever with the threat of terrorism, we cannot relax our vigilance over the threat of those Reds overrunning everything. As a hopeful future American citizen, I feel it is my duty to report this situation to the Department of Homeland Security in exchange for a green card. The un-American behavior of the Chinati Foundation is further revealed in their refusal to let a leading citizen, Martha Stewart, land her helicopter on the tennis court of the foundation on the flimsy excuse that the loose arrangement of stones, clearly copied from her Winter show on rustic arrangements, is a work of art.

Finally let me say that you should do something about the train whistles. It is unchristian the way they keep hardworking folk up at night with their air-raid alarm klaxons. Might I suggest the shrill sound be replaced by the calming sounds of *Merry Christmas from Wayne Newton?*

I thank you for your time.

Peeved Tourist, Los Angeles

A Way to Turn This to Light

There are stories told. Old stories.
        How when real men die, elders call them
back from darker shores, with only the moon to witness.
        Returned, eyes either completely black or white, blind,
they see only what light they carry inside them.
        Placing a tombstone on the corpse's crown, the old say:
Death is but our own burden, only we must carry it.

Body stiff, limbs cold and jerky, the corpse,
        grave marker on head,
                walks tirelessly into the night,
        kept in check only by
the oldest woman in the village lighting his way,
        the oldest man closing the rear.
            They alone know death
                but don't fear it.

      —-

Don't try to follow this macabre procession
        as they fade into that good night.
We all must have our day. But this one
        is shrouded in a mystery deeper than a swamp.
And the bobbing lantern holding back
        hungry shadows may be a jack-o'-lantern,
a phantom leading you to night.
                And the silence.

\-\-

Thresholds. And –
      Doors.   Doors.   Doors.

But without the hinge there is nothing
      but space and more void.
Not this, nor that; the cleft in the universe
      is the careless fold where light becomes sound.
This is where God, the hinge, resides.

\-\-

And this is what Passover is.
      The blood emblem of the lamb.
That sometimes death, unlike the meter guy,
      does come unannounced.
But in this vicious streak,
         blood and all.

\-\-

      The moment is fire.

           The moment is fire.

Refugees

There are crows here, Father,

        there are crows.

And a cathedral rising from the marsh
        of an unnamed project in an unnamed American city.

Refugees gather like so much undecided pain
        to sit in an agonized waiting
                for something that may or may not
come. This is the task.

But how can one doorway lead only to another?
Each threshold a question never answered.
Yet Father knows secrets can change you, says:
Don't dig up old bones!

What is this sanctity here?
A staircase winds down in harsh-lit concrete
and grime, to a pool of piss and a mattress
long forgotten by any back.

And a child
        huddled in the stairwell
plucking reluctant scales from the iron railing,
calling for a more expansive light.

Harare

*his thoughts shed tears for what his people
have lost.*
             Chirikure Chirikure

— —

Downtown Harare. Pavements and nice trim
islands feel like the white Africa it used to be.
Its fading beauty arrested in the late seventies
feels like Lagos in the fade of colonialism.

— —

But Yvonne says: Butterflies are burning.

    Here.

        This is kwela.

— —

In the Quill Club, black journalists hold court,
say, Bob uses this land as his
private safari. The kudus are
nearly extinct. They play pool, chafing
against the government. We could be in
The Kings Head in Finsbury Park; a cold

London night. And the locals complaining
over warm pints about the native problem.

                    ——

The still young woman smoking
            a pipe against the wall of the museum
was once a guerrilla. Says, The men here fear me.
            She knows all about killing.
Also about blowing smoke rings.

            This is kwela.

                    ——

In a market adjacent the poorest township
I finger useless trinkets, displaced as any tourist.
All the while ogling valuable-in-the-West
weathered barbershop signs
that I am too afraid to ask for.

                    ——

Everywhere people wear cosmopolitan selves
but tired, like jaded jazz singers reconciled to loss.
Hats are perched at that jaunty angle that makes you
think that all washed-out things, like Cuba, are cooler
than they are. Is this kitsch?

——

And everyone says: The trouble with Bob is…

And this is kwela.

——

In the Book Café, a vibrant subculture:
Art, music, and poetry are alive and well.
Rich whites slum with Africans: for a moment
we all believe it is possible. This. Here. Now.

——

A Rasta in Bata shoes does the twist
                    to a Beach Boys tune played by
a balding white man in a nightclub.

This is kwela.

——

The older white farmer in the five-star hotel
                    still calls this country Rhodesia.
Says, No offense, but you bloody Africans
                    can't run anything right.
I have him removed.

—–

It was not always so,
              and still I have questions.
Yes. Yes. Even this

        is kwela.

Walcott

Above hot tin billboards, above
Hostería del Mar. Along Cape Cod,
salt crannies of white harbors. At the Queen's Park
Hotel, with its white, high-ceilinged rooms
Autumn's music grates. From tuning forks of branches

Chicago's avenues, as white as Poland
Gold dung and urinous straw
from the horse garages. Certain
things here are quietly American —

Gulls bicker with the spray, while the frigate birds circle
I can sense it coming from far, too, Maman,
the tide. My double, tired of morning, closes the door
To betray philosophy is the gentle treason
Rest, Christ! from tireless war.

Two

Word for word,
* we beat the love*
out of each other.

Yusef Komunyakaa

Buffalo Women

I

Dearest Jane,

Even as I pen this, the train is whistling into the depot
bearing fresh fodder for this mad, mad war.
That sound, melancholy, like a lost starling,
always accompanies the gentle fall of evening.
Candles are rationed and our wicks are no more,
the last of the light is my only illumination as I write,
fast as a field hand racing against the coming dark.
Were that you were here, no doubt my very soul, not
just my tent, should be illumined by the gentle fire
of your affections. I have been compelled
by the argument and the insistence of my commanding
officer to leave my all negro platoon and follow him
to his new posting as the Captain of an all white platoon.
Imagine that Jane, the only negro amongst all that white
and them never guessing my deeper secret.
Our orders are to proceed to the front,
though I wish they were to repair home to you,
to the more natural plodding of my past.
Sweet Jane, I feel myself much changed
by the heady scent of sweat and dried
blood that settles like a fog over our camp.
The frenzy of killing is a delirium that drives us,
relentless as my old master's cracker drove me. My

love, it was not my intent to let this vulgar life into the more gentle innocence of yours. Remember always that I love you.

Sincerely,
Henri

II

Dear Henri,

Your letters are more precious than life to me.
They do much to assuage my fear of losing you,
though it is never fully allayed. The space between
each one is like a slow agonizing death, and I
worry for you so. Why insist on this stubbornness?
You have only to reveal your mortal wound to the medics
and they will discharge you unto me.
You may still receive a pension, and no matter if not,
we have always managed with the farm.
I cannot imagine the terrifying spectacles
that you are witness to, although in your sweetness
you do try to share them – your words betray the difficulty.
Promise me that you will strive always to be safe.
Remember the bird of paradise you planted?
Well it has spread in the garden, so that it looks as though
a gaggle of tropical birds have gone berserk.
It would amuse you nearly as much as the time the jacaranda
trees coated the front yard in a carpet of lavender petals,
and you rolling in them for hours.
I am enclosing some rags to stanch your blood
and a long piece of sheet to swaddle yourself.

Hurry home my love,
Jane

III

Dearest Jane,

Flesh is a curious thing. To the eye
it does appear seamless and in that thinking stronger
than any metal. Yet this wondrous creation, once
the seam is ripped, lets out all the fluid of its living
absorbing instead death. The way a fish on land fears
the emptying of water, draws in air. The impulse to be filled,
to be full of something, anything, seems to drive this odd
beast. Yesterday I killed my first man.
Rammed my bayonet into him with such ferocity,
that I drove him back five feet. Dropping his rifle,
he opened his mouth in surprise as death filled him.
And I loved it. The trembling that began in my stomach,
rushed up to the back of my head, then down to the rise of
my pubes. Causing the hair to rise deliciously. It felt
wholesome, profound. The epiphany, like the taste of
blood on the tongue. Or earth. Dank. Damp.
Later, behind some bushes, as I hunched to change rags
and burn the old one, I wiped the still bleeding blade
of my bayonet, feeling the trembling return,
stronger this time, as my blood mingled
with that of the soldiers who had died at its point.
This feeling, Jane, was something new, something feral,
like the single purpose of a single moment.

Yours truly,
Henri

Sweetest Henri,

I know we promised to be honest,
one to the other, but your recent missive,
though welcome as any epistle from you,
filled me with a dread that clung
like dampness to wet wood. I am terrified
for your immortal soul, dear sweet Henri.
This mad war of Lincoln's is infecting you
with a sickness too depraved to even address.
I have gathered in some herbs,
remembered from childhoods with my Aunt Tilly.
I will use them to spice the candles I light
every night with my prayers. I must be careful
because, whilst they are wholesome with my love,
there are those who will tar it witchcraft.
God knows we need no more stigmas attached to us,
or for the town to examine us more closely.
Yesterday, Rev. Pickering spoke highly of your manhood;
it was all I could do to keep from laughing.
The Wilson farm was raided,
marauders slaughtering every living creature.
They were a sight, scattered there like the senseless
pieces of a broken vase. To avert the same fate,
I sold our creatures, buying gold dust in their stead,
which I hid in the stem of your pipe.
It lies there, forlorn, a wretch awaiting its master.

Some evenings I sit before the fire, puffing
on its unlit stem, my lips to yours.

Always your heart,
Jane

V

Dearest Sweet Jane,

I woke with the taste of your apple pie in my mouth,
carried over no doubt from my dreams.
It made me realize how much I miss you and our home.
Though I think that dreams are really the place
for such memories, as my old life seems
to be no more than a dream. Being
up earlier than everyone else, a gift made
possible by the dream of you, I was able to wash
in the river naked. Removing all my garments and bindings,
I felt my body sigh like a flower opening to the sun.
The relief of it was immeasurable.
I sank gratefully into the embrace of the water,
the break between the surface and depth of it
producing tiny waves, like a mouth kissing my nipples.
Teasing the way you always do, first with your hair
then your lips, remember? I confess that my hand
found my tenderness and the release
was like the sun on water.
I have been thinking, my love, and on my return,
I would like to reveal the truth of us, of myself.
I am tired of this restrictive masculine role.
Write soon, my love.

Yours truly,
Henri

VI

My Sweet Henri,

I do feel very guilty. So much
time has elapsed since your last letter.
It is the fault of a wicked illness making the rounds,
once infected it seems impossible to shake
the clammy hand of death it brings.
Mrs. Wilcox has passed from it, as has the young
Harding boy. I thought it best to stay put and not
venture into town. Making a reply impossible to post.
I find myself going to church more these days,
to beseech that you be kept safe. I know
you will scoff at this, but it brings me much comfort
so I will continue to do it. Repeat Psalm 23 daily.
My Aunt Tilly used to take a decoction of dried
St. John's Wort, a curious but amazing root.
I am enclosing some here. It raises the spirit
and I have much hope it will help you by and by.
I know hope is indeed too unformed a thing to ask
you to hold on to, but at times like these, it is the best
we can ask for ourselves. I have enough hope
for us both, my love. I flushed when I read
your last letter and confess I return to it on retiring
most nights. I miss you terribly, my heart, and keep a lamp
lit every night in the window to guide you home,
safe and with a heart of love.

Your wife,
Jane

VII

Dear Jane,

I read somewhere that the world we see is new
only once, in the innocence of infancy.
The rest is just the recall of memory.
Were that it were true, I would not feel like
the wretch I know I am become.
This infernal conflict is no place for a soul
as delicate as mine, and I say that while
still claiming the equal of any man.
Now, more than before, I realize that we cannot
but be changed by it, learning new things daily.
Constantly the natural world around us, and
the impure stain of our own nature,
acts upon us so as to make us this way.
I killed more men today. Not with the distance
of a musket shot or the justice of a sword.
This was something entirely different.
I clubbed them to death with my rifle stock.
Beat them with the confidence of a Chinese
washerwoman. Until their bodies yielded
red to my cleansing. All the time,
I grunted, moaned even. The sound low
and sweet at the back of my throat. Clubbing
until each one was still, then panting.
I gulped for air, sweating, alive, so alive.
Then laughing like a coyote circling something

dying slowly in the desert, I took a deep breath
and moved forward. The killing never stops.
I am afraid of what I am becoming, Jane.

Henri

VIII

Dear Jane,

It has been a while since your last letter
and I am worried about you. Where are you?
I am kept awake by my fear that
something unspeakable has befallen you.
I am keeping as well as I can, given the circumstances
here. We are trapped, pinned down on one side
by the weather – snow and a frozen river
that may not bear the full burden –
and on the other by the hatred of the enemy,
which is preferable to the indifference of snow.
We have taken some heavy cannons and
the horizon is filled with splintered trees grinning
like teeth in a skull. To give you a true sense
of the troubling scenes I have witnessed is beyond
my power and I scarce think you would believe me.
Suffice it to say that the devil returns
among us nightly, dancing between the tents
of freezing hungry men. In the lazy sunlight of day,
there is much talk too evil to recount here,
taking shape in covetous stares aimed at the old, weak
and dying. There is something malevolent brewing
in our very souls. A thing so heinous
that should we wish to return from it, we could not
devise a path home. With a growing dread,

I realize that I am not immune from it.
Pray for my immortal soul, sweet Jane. Pray!

Yours truly,
Henri

IX

Dearest Jane,

I have not heard from you in a long time,
nor you from me. I realize
that we are sealed off by weather and the war
as surely as though we were butterflies
wrapped in the silk of those cocoons you love
so, calling them beautiful, holy.
We are all dizzy from hunger here, and emaciated.
So wasted have I become that I no longer need
my chest binding. I am truly one of the men.
You would not recognize me, my love.
My face is harrowing even to crows.
The older and dying soldiers have been tagged
crones by the rest of us. We watch them
with guarded eyes and they can feel it coming.
This hunger that must take shape soon.
They huddle together like ancient birds,
eyes darting, calculating every movement we make.
And daily our circle about them grows tighter,
pulled by the spasms of hunger-taut bellies.
So far, it is only the shame of daylight, and night
fires that keep it in. But how long before
this desperate wickedness overruns the qualms
of good people? Before the desire for the smell
of cooking meat, the softness of flesh, breaks us all?
This is an unspeakable horror, Jane,

and I would surely be hanged for telling you.
You will never read this and for that, I am grateful.

Yours truly,
Henri

X

Dear Jane,

I suspect this letter will never feel
the gentle grace of your hands,
nor will you read these words.
The snow shows no signs of letting up,
and the cold is worse even than the night terrors,
its icy hold claiming fingers and limbs as though
devouring us one appendage at a time.
My wound has dried up, the flow no doubt frozen
by this infernal weather or perhaps even the hunger.
We have begun to boil our spare boots along with salt
and the few spices Cook has left.
The leather is too tough to eat, but the soup
has enough of the taste of meat to fool our hunger
momentarily. We bulk up on tree bark.
Today we made a charge at the enemy.
It was halfhearted and we failed
to do more than drive them a few yards back.
But they too are so debilitated
they could not mount a successful counter.
Neither side it seems can muster the mettle to succeed.
We always return to the problem of finding food.
All the horses and mules are long gone,
the marrow picked clean from the bones.
I swear one can play them like a flute.
Even the crows have deserted us in fear.

Today our captain gave a rousing speech about how
it was our duty to stay alive and enjoined us not to falter
in that duty. The abyss is calling, sweet Jane.

Henri

XI

Dearest Jane,

And this is how it is done.
We chased down the oldest crone last night.
It was no sport, and despite their sprightliness
born of terror, the hunt took only a few moments.
The other crones all pulled tight into balls,
dark stones in the purity of snow. Even in the dark,
we could see the widening of the crone's eyes,
the recognition that pleading was futile.
Four men held it down, ripping its clothes off.
It was no more than a bag of bones, but to us it was plump
as a new calf. Its squirming and pig-like
squeals enjoined no pity from us, but a desperate anger.
We circled in clumps of two's and three's, hugging
the shadows as far from the fire as possible.
Our shame compounded by hunger and anger
and then mercifully the sergeant ran his sword through
the crone, slicing from chest to navel,
viscera steaming in the snow.
The Chaplin and Captain turned away in disgust.
But what could they do? The confusion
that followed was suddenly comical;
nobody knew how to cook it.
Our curse is our endless resourcefulness for evil
and the night was soon heavy
with the deliciousness of cooking meat,

and while the crone dripped fat into the fire,
we mimicked the noises it made before dying.
And so we have become.

Henri

XII

Dearest Jane,

I received my first letter from you
in nearly three months. I cannot measure my joy
at your tender words. Along with your letter,
spring has thawed winter's internment
and we have moved even farther forward.
Our resourcefulness allowed us to find food
during the winter months while the enemy starved
for the lack of it. We were able to launch attack
after attack on them. We left the dead where they fell,
and now in spring's thaw they have emerged from the snow
like the wanton pieces of the broken jar your missive speaks of.
There were casualties on our side too,
but nothing near the losses suffered by the South.
The Chaplin and Captain recommended our battalion
be disbanded and the soldiers sent to new postings.
This last winter was harsh on our conscience
and everyone feels it best to forget.
I wrote you several letters in that long darkness,
none of which survived to be sent to you.
I laughed when I read of you puffing on my unlit pipe
stuffed with gold-dust. What a remarkable creature you are.
I have decided that I want no more of this war,
and revealed myself to the doctor whose lust

weighed my breasts before discharging me.
I will be home soon. You are my redemption, sweet Jane.

Yours truly,
Henrietta

Three

here every discovery is intense and fragile
Roland Barthes

Hands Washing Water

Even in the falling
a train breaks for the light.
The tunnel, the darkness – never

sweeter. This body is not
real. Yet living.
This living body.

There is a child. The blessed
coolness of water.
And hands

Fire

Lost, but for the flames we drag
through dark streets; smoke and dust
Aho je la, aho je la, aho jengeje, aho jengeje
This chant is sky orotund with sun
and the mirage: a pot smoldering
against night's face, startling last year's
spirits gathering in corners, holding on.
And this: The crackle of burning firewood,
a train of palm fronds like hungry tongues
licking the street, parched from the intensity.
Beyond the brood of dark hills the sea;
salt and stone. This is not superstition.
This is how we write love.

Lacan

What is this vanity of words?

What chance this?

      A cello full of sea. And tea
steaming a winter window.

The New Religion

The body is a nation I have not known.
The pure joy of air: the moment between leaping
from a cliff into the wall of blue below. Like that.
Or to feel the rub of tired lungs against skin-
covered bone, like a hand against the rough of bark.
Like that. "The body is a savage," I said.
For years I said that: the body is a savage.
As if this safety of the mind were virtue
not cowardice. For years I have snubbed
the dark rub of it, said, "I am better, Lord,
I am better," but sometimes, in an unguarded
moment of sun, I remember the cowdung-scent
of my childhood skin thick with dirt and sweat
and the screaming grass.
But this distance I keep is not divine,
for what was Christ if not God's desire
to smell his own armpit? And when I
see him, I know he will smile,
fingers glued to his nose, and say, "Next time
I will send you down as a dog
to taste this pure hunger."

The Measure of Sorrow

Fireflies caught in a jar die.
A child mourns the passing light.
Your father dies, your name on his lips
Each syllable a curse. Or so you imagine.
A clumsy salsa, all left feet with your lover
Never finding the right cadence,
A filterless cigarette burning and the café
Facing the river on a cold Parisian
Evening cannot bear the weight.
What words can be said to rain and night
And a car speeding through both?
Three lines stolen from you, old gypsy,
Magician at his own revival
Here are all the shadows that have fallen,
A single window smashed and bare with sky.

Aphasia

My language is dying the same way

      my father did:

Alone. Night. And there are no storms. Only

      moonlight straining through holes in a tin roof

And the slight exhalation, lips

      pursed as though to say: *Uwa'm.*

The Old Artist Speaks to the Young Poet

Each visitation changes something.
Let the angel go and climb the ladder.
There is God in this effort. This thing
is more existential, only not desire.
To the left, metal assemblage leans lazily
into rust. He runs arthritic hands
over its rough. You always work
with something, he says. This is
an actual horse's leg. Nicely weathered.
Why if it weren't for the nails it would run away
with the picture. Chagall would like that.
A blank television regards me –
The news and the weather, he says.
With time, he says, everything dissolves into art

from There Are No Names For Red

A taxi through night and palms that gather desire like the dew.
A window opens onto the hiss of rain on tarmac and this smell
is old earth, and a grave, grace even, and flowers rotting
at the edge of time, at the edge of the road where a child died.
It's like the way the little white plane hovers on the vastness of
the ocean between Godthåb and Saint John's. The Atlantic tamed
momentarily by the flight- information screen; and yet in the
    dark cabin,
all that keeps it aloft is the soft breathing of the other sleeping
    passengers.
And nothing is lonelier in the world at this moment
than that little white cross on the expanse of blue screen.
Faith is something like this, I imagine. Not of God. But of a pen
    or a brush
held up like the last flaming torch of the century, and yet flimsy —
this desire of the artist to keep the blue from swallowing it all up.
Like something that happens only at night.
Like a lie and desperation so thick you can breathe it. Moments
like this, the skin widens to the lover's touch and the back arches
    to whispers.
Even this cannot keep the void away. The Mid-Atlantic Ridge is a
mountain under the sea, and its active volcanoes widen the
    ocean bed.
I want to say, "This one's on me, Mr. Freud! Can I get an Amen?"
Still we're lost in that vast blue and I think how did the Vikings
    ever find

anything down there? Stumbling about in the dark like still-
    unrealized ids.

There is nothing clear about it, nothing lasting about this clarity.

"I will do it different," I say. I will. As if the threat of death is
    not a smell

I will lose in a few days. This terror comes in without knocking.

Like a familiar lover intruding into the bathroom as I pee.

I will lose even this when it mingles with the old smell of her
    wetness

and I will forget and drown us both in wine and regret.

Coleman

Ornette Coleman didn't play no cornet.
But he played the saxophone, guitar,
drums, violin, and on occasion, trumpet.
But Coleman was no whole man
'cos he snipped off the things they say
make a man play rough
'cos he say it mek 'im play sof'.
If Coleman had lived in the South
when black men garnished trees
he would have got his operation for free – see?

Low-down Dirty Blues

This is a shame I can get behind
like the thick molasses scent of
a no-man's-blues. Which is not grace.
What can I say? I have French-kissed sorrow,
but there is an intimacy deeper still.
They say the beautiful changes; but not always
contained in the ease of modal shifts, okay Miles?
Altogether different. This is desire. This is song.

Foucault's Funk

And staring into the thick black of her coffee
she reads a future that hangs on the balance
of the fast-forward button of a VCR
and smoke from her cigarette rises to God
sitting in the office above behind a new IBM desktop
and she waves her hands in mandalas as she hums
to the background ritual chants of L.A.
and Babyface
and then she says that life's a bitch
and across the room a young man snorts some coke
and collapses into rapture
and mumbles yeah I'm scared yeah cool man cool
and still she reads my future
and that of all humanity as she waves the cigarette
and espouses the advances of science
and did I know that they had split the atom
and that tetrapyloctomy was the art of splitting a hair into four
and did I know that life was happier now that we had cars
and airplanes that lent wings to man's dreams
and outside the window I watch a dog sneak up on a fire
        hydrant like Humphrey in an old B —
and I say to her read me a future full of hope
and she smiles as if she thought it some funny joke, then:
        we are lucky to live *now,* I mean, look how far we've come.

Morning Yet:

God,
pinching between forefinger and thumb
rolls the night up into a long joint.
The match rasps; his face
glows as he cups it from the wind

Ode to a Rag

Wounded with a blessing, he says. But how
do you begin to talk about your life, your art?
It's just that deep, he says. Just that deep.

The broken back of sincerity, he says. There.
Grass, reaching for the sun, pushing through
concrete. *That* cannot be talked about.

Imagine, to rove these neighborhoods, where
trees, skeletal like telephone poles, are silent.
And to tie brightly colored rags, spreading, spreading,
covert, unsigned, a pure gift to life. There.

But see, you know, you know, he says,
what a thing – to wake to that explosion of desire,
warming yourself in the need of your children.
It's just that deep, he says. Just that deep.

Letter to the President

Death is silent like this stone
Death is silent like this stone
Death is silent like this stone
Death is silent like this stone
Death is silent like this stone
Death is silent like this stone
Death is silent like this stone
Death is silent like this stone

Death is nothing like this stone
Death is nothing like this stone
Death is nothing like this stone
Death is nothing like this stone
Death is nothing like this stone
Death is nothing like this stone

Say Something about Child's Play

The soldier asks the boy: Choose which
do I cleave? Your right arm or left?
The boy, ten, maybe nine, says: Neither,
or when I play, like a bird with a broken wing
I will smudge the line of the hopscotch
square, let the darkness in.

The soldier asks again: Choose which
do I cleave? Your right leg or left?
Older in this moment than his dead father, the boy
says: Neither, or when I dance the spirit dance,
I will stumble, kick sand in the face of light.

This boy says: Take my right eye,
it has seen too much, but leave me the left,
I will need it to see God.

Ouija Board

A road chasing a horizon
A morning to believe
A candle, flame wavering, wavering
A pebble. Dreaming of mountains
A rock in the sun
A dead man in a phone box, holding
A busy signal, the tone of purgatory
A sower, sweat, and the denseness of clay
A death of hyenas
A lone footprint in the sand: Tuesday
A train in an iris
A bullet surprising flesh with its sting
A person is what we dream
The sky doesn't die. It is only night, child.

War Widow

The telephone never rings. Still
you pick it up, smile into the static,
the breath of those you've loved; long dead.

The leaf you pick from the fall
rises and dips away with every ridge.
Fingers stiff from time, you trace.

Staring off into a distance limned
by cataracts and other collected debris,
you have forgotten none of the long-ago joy
of an ice-cream truck and its summer song.

Between the paving stones;
between tea, a cup, and the sound
of you pouring;
between the time you woke that morning
and the time when the letter came,
a tired sorrow: like an old flagellant
able only to tease with a weak sting.

Riding the elevator all day,
floor after floor after floor,
each stop some small victory whittled
from the hard stone of death, you smile.
They used to write epics about moments like this.

Skin

Soft.

Then fire.

Muir Woods

In this Cathedral Grove, trees rise in devotion
older than words. In the red-tinted light
stands a woman in a black yashmak. Only her
eyes are visible and they lock onto a black-tailed deer,
its red coat fanning through the green. Her hands fly
to her mouth to contain the rush, but the words are out.
Every man turns toward the delicate husk; her voice.
And her husband's face betrays the knowledge.
This is how God unstitches our fear.

A Warrior's Pride

Wet the whetstone
fetch water from the stream.
Clean the broadsword
fetch a kitchen rag, rich with soot & ash.
This is how we hone the blade.

        Stone.

Place the blade flat and draw
back. Watch your limbs.
Flat and draw
Flat and draw
        Water.
Draw and flat
Draw and flat
        Grass.
Only one blade dropped
across the steel's new smile.
If it splits apart, it is done.
            If not

      begin again.

Place the blade flat and draw
        Water.
        Grass.

Turn it over. Hone the twin edge.
Take care in the curve.
A lazy turn and the blade will skitter across
        wet stone
           drink deep
                of your blood.
Heed this! A blade will fulfill its destiny.

Hold the sword up to the light.
Watch it flaunt in the sun.
This is a warrior's pride.

The drawn metal must be fed.
        Untie the goat from its tether.
Slap its rump with the flat of the blade.
        Let it begin to run.
                Catch up to it in five strides.
Take its head with one quick swing.
          Listen to the blade sigh.
       This is a warrior's pride.

          Grandfather says:
Heed this! A severed head cannot be put back.
       This is a warrior's wisdom.

Howl

If this is the curse, then what is the sin?
This is a land, deep red and baked hard by hate.
And though blessings can seem immediate, rude even,
every despair is more existential yet essential here.
Don't blame the bard, don't. The wind is his kin.

Sankara! And another train disappears into night
and shadow. In this afternoon, light—
heavy as ripe fruit. Taste this loam here.
Dark, thick, and sweet as any rum cake. But wait.

To say: This way we suffer is harder than. The plight?
Like trying to catch the blue heart of a moving flame
as the candle drips wax into a measure, even.
Or nothing. Or something. This surely though is grace:
an African child dying, smile stretched thin, even white.

Secrets

Through the keyhole and spreading rapidly
like a shadow or light which is a brighter
shadow and the eye struggling skin cold
against metal and the hoping to see and then
a fragment of a word lost down there on the floor
where light from a lamp patterns in slivers
the disapproval and even the goose bumps
crawling up your skin and the licking
of chocolate off the baking spoon never tasted
this good and then the muted rustling of cloth
and the slap slap of slippers clapping against
the wood floor and even the rug is a jungle
and still the metal cold around an eye straining
to see and the sound which is a whisper travels
up your body to lodge just beneath the skin
which bumps and shivers and the pulling away
is the door swinging open onto shame.

The Cleft in the Infinite

:

;

How We Come to Name

Bricking up the window, one

      stone displaced, as if

even this despair is not all, or all.

      Light turning to stone —

This we call star.

Unfinished Symphony

The light this morning is an aria.
        I turn back to the stirring of coffee.
A way to ground this time
        between the hush and the turning. Outside
a hummingbird is spreading rumors
        among flowers. Even now.
Even after all the wounds have healed,
        I scratch around a phantom scab, avoiding
what lies beneath. When I open the window,
        rosemary and thyme spill in.
Later I will work loam in the herb garden,
        crumbling the dirt, whispering dirges,
spicing the plants with sharpness. For now,
        there is Percival's painted fire
and the coffee. Sometimes
                    it is enough.

Notes

"Auckland" is for Michele Leggott.

"Antwerp" is for Gerd Segers.

"Durban, South Africa – Some Notations of Value" is for Keorapetse "Willie" Kgositsile.

"Hanging in Egypt with Breyten Breytenbach" is for Basma, Hanane, Rabab, Mona, Miret, and Breyten Breytenbach.

"Poem" is for Frank O'Hara.

"Letter to the Editor" is for Kristen, Douglas, and the people of Marfa, Texas.

"Refugees" is for Lucille Clifton.

"Harare" is for Yvonne Vera, Chirikure Chirikure, and Freedom.

"Walcott" is after Terrance Hayes. This poem is made up of lines and partial lines found in the index of first lines in Derek Walcott's *Midsummer.* Terrance Hayes's book *Hip Logic* opens with a similar poem ("Lorde") made up of lines from the index of *The Collected Poems of Audre Lorde,* under *W.*

"Buffalo Women": This section of the book explores the correspondence between Henrietta and girlfriend Jane, a gay couple living together in the California area during the Civil War. Henrietta/Henri is a recently emancipated slave, and Jane is a white woman from the South. Such relationships did exist at the time, and it was not uncommon during the Civil War for women to pretend to be men in order to enlist to fight. There is also documentation that many troops came from the California area. Troops were segregated, with all-black corps having white officers. However, in "Buffalo Woman" Henri is the only soldier of color in an all-white company, the aide-de-camp of the Captain.

"Fire" is for Bei Dao.

"The Measure of Sorrow" is for Larry Levis. The last three lines of this poem are by Larry Levis and are taken from *The Selected Levis.*

"Aphasia" is for Michael Echeruo. *Uwa'm* translates as "my world." But in Igbo it is also understood to be a phrase, "my goodness." It also means, "my life," "my destiny"; it can also be a lament. This is not exhaustive. At death, it is, quite literally, "giving up the ghost."

"The Old Artist Speaks to the Young Poet" is for Noah Purifoy.

"Coleman": Ornette Coleman, saxophonist and free-jazz exponent of the late sixties and early seventies, was rumored to have had a voluntary castration operation to improve his playing.

"Low-down Dirty Blues" is for Walter Mosley.

"Ode to a Rag" is for John Outterbridge.

"Letter to the President" is for Horikawa Michio, a Japanese artist who in 1969, in response to the Apollo 11 mission, collected pebbles and stones from the Shinano River and sent them to eleven world leaders, including President Nixon, with a letter stating, "Nothing changes in the universe if humanity stood on the Moon and brought back stones. What does change is humanity and his thinking." This project he called *The Shinano River Plan 11*.

"Say Something about Child's Play" is for Yusef Komunyakaa.

"Ouija Board" is for David St. John.

"War Widow" is for Guillaume Apollinaire.

"Skin" is for Blair (Obi).

"A Warrior's Pride" is for Idume Chukwu, clan father.

"Howl" is for Odia Ofeimun. Thomas Sankara was the revolutionary socialist head of state of Burkina Faso, assassinated in 1987.

"The Cleft in the Infinite" is for John Cage.

"Unfinished Symphony" is for Percival Everett.

About the Author

Chris Abani is an associate professor at the University of California–Riverside. He is the recipient of the PEN USA Freedom to Write Award, the Prince Claus Award, a Lannan Literary Fellowship, a California Book Award, a Hurston/Wright Legacy Award, and the Hemingway Foundation/PEN Award.

The Chinese character for poetry is made up of two parts: "word" and "temple." It also serves as pressmark for Copper Canyon Press. Founded in 1972, Copper Canyon Press remains dedicated to publishing poetry exclusively, from Nobel laureates to new and emerging authors. The Press thrives with the generous patronage of readers, writers, booksellers, librarians, teachers, students, and funders—everyone who shares the conviction that poetry invigorates the language and sharpens our appreciation of the world.

Major funding has been provided by:

Anonymous (2)

The Paul G. Allen Family Foundation

Lannan Foundation

National Endowment for the Arts

Washington State Arts Commission

For information and catalogs:

COPPER CANYON PRESS
Post Office Box 271
Port Townsend, Washington 98368
360-385-4925
www.coppercanyonpress.org

*Set in Mendoza, a typeface designed by
José Mendoza y Almeida. Book design and
composition by Valerie Brewster, Scribe Typography.
Printed on archival-quality Glatfelter Author's Text
at McNaughton & Gunn, Inc.*